IKIGAI

生き甲斐

IKIGAI

—

Discover Your Reason for Being

Justyn Barnes

QUARTO PRESS

Inspiring | Educating | Creating | Entertaining

Brimming with creative inspiration, how-to projects, and useful
information to enrich your everyday life, Quarto Knows is a favourite
destination for those pursuing their interests and passions. Visit our
site and dig deeper with our books into your area of interest:
Quarto Creates, Quarto Cooks, Quarto Homes, Quarto Lives,
Quarto Drives, Quarto Explores, Quarto Gifts, or Quarto Kids.

First Published in 2018 by Quarto Press,
and imprint of The Quarto Group.
The Old Brewery, 6 Blundell Street,
London N7 9BH, United Kingdom.
T (0)20 7700 6700 F (0)20 7700 8066
www.QuartoKnows.com

ISBN: 978-1-78131-829-4

QUAR.306732

Editor: Anna Southgate
Designer: Dave Jones
Senior Art Editor: Emma Clayton
Editorial Assistant: Cassie Lawrence
Publisher: Samantha Warrington

Printed in China

MIX
Paper from
responsible sources
FSC® C104723
FSC
www.fsc.org

CONTENTS

INTRODUCTION

Are you leading a comfortable life, but feel there is something missing? Or is day-to-day life an endless struggle? Are you wondering how you ended up where you are, or where you are heading? Perhaps you just haven't found your ikigai yet.

The Japanese term *ikigai* (pronounced 'eek-ee-guy') has no direct English translation, but, in simple terms, it describes 'value in living' or 'reason for living'. It is the amalgamation of two words: *iki* (to live), and *gai* (which describes value, worth or reason). There are myriad interpretations of ikigai's meaning, even among Japanese people who habitually use the word. Here is just a small selection: joy and a sense of well-being from being alive; a

reason to jump out of bed every morning; realising the value of being alive; useful purpose; your current aim; the object – for example, a person, job or possession – that makes your life worth living; a subjective happy feeling; and, my personal favourite, a springboard for tomorrow.

In essence ikigai is about living a personally meaningful life that truly expresses your inner self. It is about making the most of every day, rooted in the belief that finding fulfilment in many things, both large and small, is the secret to a more rewarding life, rather than extrinsic measures of success, such as wealth or social status. The sense of purpose derived from pursuing ikigai will also bolster your resilience so that you can overcome setbacks and feel positive about your future.

This book explores the nuances of ikigai, with parables from everyday life, inspiring quotations and practical tips to show how to enjoy a healthier, more satisfying life. It will help you identify your own ikigai and to live your best life.

Justyn Barnes

1

ASPECTS OF IKIGAI

Start your journey with some
perspectives on ikigai and examples
of ways in which it has guided
and benefitted Japanese people.

SEVEN NEEDS

Japanese psychiatrist Mieko Kamiya identified seven key needs associated with ikigai: a fulfilling existence; change and growth; future perspectives; receiving responses; freedom; self-actualisation; and significance and value. The balance of such biological, social and spiritual needs varies from individual to individual, and some of them are interlinked and may be met by following a single objective. The key is to try to achieve things that align with your true nature. When you embark on your journey, whether you fulfil your goals is relatively unimportant; it's taking steps in the right direction – the right direction for you – that counts.

Everyday life

──────

It goes without saying that a good life should include
many moments of great joy and happiness – say, the
immediate elation of reaching the peak of a mountain
or of winning a prize – but these are likely to be
relatively fleeting. In Japan, ikigai is a more highly
valued aspiration. The concept offers a more nuanced
view of well-being. Rather than strive for happiness as
an end goal, then, far better to seek meaning and
fulfilment in everyday life – the highs,
the lows and the humdrum.

6 Ikigai isn't a grand target …
it's a spectrum of small things.
The really big things might
only happen once a decade,
so life isn't sustainable
without small daily joys. 9

———

Ken Mogi, neuroscientist,
author and broadcaster

RISE AND SHINE

Ikigai is sometimes framed as 'the reason for getting up in the morning'. One of Japan's great communal pastimes is called *radio taiso* and traditionally takes place in local parks as early as 6.30am. Although people of all ages are known to practice *radio taiso*, older generations, in particular, gather to perform gentle mobilisation exercises to music broadcast on the radio. For devotees, this ritual is, in itself, an ikigai, an essential part of their lives. If you struggle to get up in the mornings, find a physical activity that motivates you to do so, and that mobilises and energises you for the day ahead.

Longevity

—

The Okinawa archipelago in Japan has a population with one of the highest overall life expectancies in the world, and a disproportionate number of centenarians living active, purposeful lives. Their longevity is attributed to a number of factors. They enjoy a healthy, varied plant-based diet and practice *har hachi bu* – eating until they are 80 per cent full. The same sense of moderation is applied to exercise, with regular light, physical activity integral to their lifestyles – that is, staying mobile, rather than going to the gym. Okinawa is also notable for its strong and cheerful community spirit founded on *yuimaaru* (teamwork) and each individual's ikigai, the inner drive to make the most of every moment.

Perfectly imperfect

The Japanese philosophy of *wabi sabi* teaches us to appreciate the innate imperfection and impermanent nature of the world around us and this idea can be helpful in our pursuit of ikigai. Say one of your ikigai is to maintain a stable, organised and happy home. Your vision of what this means will be challenged by changes and flaws in yourself and family members, outside influences and even the life cycle of household objects and appliances. Nothing is fixed, perfect or lasts forever, so rather than rage against the imperfections, quirks and idiosyncrasies you will inevitably encounter in life, find beauty in the blemishes.

PURPOSEFULLY REPURPOSED

The Venn diagram that is widely used as a basis to
explain the concept of ikigai actually had the word
'purpose' at its centre originally. Then, in 2014, Marc
Winn, a self-proclaimed 'change maker and community-
led innovation specialist', wrote a blog post about ikigai,
illustrated with the purpose diagram . . . except he
substituted in the word 'ikigai'. One changed word and
the revised meme has since been shared globally and
influenced millions of people to seek their ikigai.

6 The secret to a long
and happy life is not to
live in the hope of a great
life tomorrow. It is to live
with intention today. 9

Marc Winn, change maker
and innovation specialist

2

WHAT ARE YOU DOING AND WHY?

Where are you in life at this moment?
Unpick the complex web of personal and external
influences that brought you to this point.

The search
for meaning

Do you feel your life has meaning? What does a life with meaning even look like? Nikkyō Niwano, co-founder of the Japanese Buddhist organisation Risshō Kōsei Kai, offered his personal take in his 1969 book *Ningen no Ikigai* (*The Meaningful Life*): '. . . a meaningful life is one lived with a sense of fulfilment. A person who enjoys numerous contacts with others, is constantly active and always looks forward to something is mentally and physically vigorous. Such vitality, which makes life worthwhile, is not shallow pleasure confined to the level of consciousness. It is instead a profound, joyful awareness of the innermost reality of life'.

True colour

We are all different. Even the closest of friends or family members do not share exactly the same character traits, opinions or beliefs. To borrow the Japanese idiom *jūnin toiro* – 'ten persons, ten colours' – we all have a different colour, no matter how slight the variation. You may admire other people, hold them up as role models and learn from them, but you will always be you. Follow your ikigai and show your true colour.

The mystery of human existence lies not in just staying alive, but in finding something to live for.

Fyodor Dostoyevsky,
from *The Brothers Karamazov*

IKIGAI IN A NAPPY

In his 2018 novel *Spring*, Norwegian author Karl Ove Knausgaard draws on his personal experience of having an unexpected fourth daughter, his wife's breakdown and their subsequent divorce. He highlights the small joys that help to sustain a father through life's struggles. One such moment is the second or two when he feels the weight of his baby daughter's nappy before changing it. It tells him that his daughter's bodily functions are working, that she is healthy despite the family's issues, one indicator that he is fulfilling his duty of care as a father. What could be perceived as a minor, mundane and messy chore, takes on profound meaning. So even changing a nappy can be an ikigai.

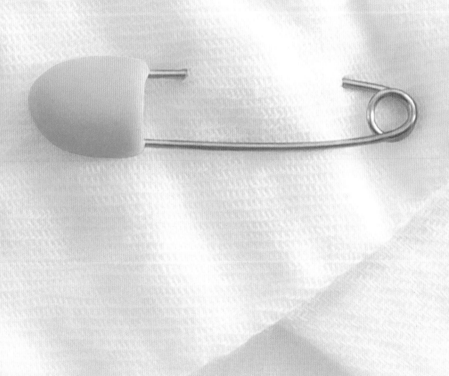

Don't wait for an elephant

Are you good at what you do, but feel you are not really doing what you should be? You are not alone. Social, cultural and economic factors prompt people to drift into situations that, while perfectly comfortable, fail to satisfy their innermost desires. Gangadharan Menon gave a TEDx Talk about his own experience. Having fallen into a career in advertising, he went on to spend 28 successful years in the sector. It was only after surviving an attack by an elephant against all odds, that he was prompted to reassess what he was doing with the life he could so easily have lost. Aged 52, Menon belatedly searched for his own true path, and has since found his ikigai in travel writing and photography. His advice? 'Don't wait for an elephant. You may not survive'.

TUNE OUT/TUNE IN

———

We are constantly bombarded with messages from companies offering products and services that claim they will improve our lives. From YouTube videos punctuated by advertisements to website articles with pop-ups that chase you down the screen as you read, corporate messaging is inescapable. Algorithms draw on your browsing history to tailor advertisements to your supposed desires and needs. Take time out to unplug, tune out the noise and tune in to your inner voice.

‟ I make sure that, occasionally, late at night, I'll have a drink or two, not think about anything in front of me but just sit back and think about my life: How's it going? What's bothering me? What's really going on now? ”

Gordon Mathews, professor of anthropology, Chinese University of Hong Kong

ACCEPTANCE OF MORTALITY

In 2009, Bronnie Ware wrote a blog post called 'The Top Five Regrets of the Dying', based on her experience as a palliative nurse. It struck a chord with people around the world and spawned a bestselling memoir. One lesson Ware drew from the people she cared for in their final days was the importance of accepting mortality early on in life. We often postpone such thoughts until actually faced with death, and as a consequence don't follow our ikigai until it is too late. Ware believes that acknowledging we have a limited time on this planet 'offers us the opportunity to find greater purpose and satisfaction in the time we have remaining'.

3
WHAT
YOU LOVE

Love links to your passion and mission.
How can you harness your love for
activities, objects and people to add
new layers of meaning to your life?

FIND YOUR FLOW

Do you ever get so engrossed in an activity that you lose
all sense of time, are focused solely on the here and now
and immune to all distractions? It is at such times that
you release your ego and achieve flow. The pleasure you
feel comes purely from what you are doing, without any
need for financial reward or recognition from others.
You can observe flow in a young child playing with
a favourite toy. Doing something you love in this
psychological state is bliss. But imagine if you could
achieve flow in relatively mundane everyday tasks. Well,
this is possible too when you realise that they are part of
your ikigai – that which makes your life meaningful.

Beware
obsessive passion

———

Passion is a powerful motivational force for human beings, but you need to be aware that you can express 'obsessive' passion as well as 'harmonious' passion. Obsessive passion is when you feel an uncontrollable urge to participate in an activity you view as important or enjoyable. The problem is that you get frustrated when prevented from doing this activity. Equally, if you spend excessive time on the activity while neglecting, say, pressing work- or family-related commitments, you feel distracted and cannot possibly achieve the flow state. Dissatisfaction reigns.

Embrace
harmonious passion

———

If you express 'harmonious passion' for an activity,
you have control. You *choose* to engage in the activity you
love, rather than feel an uncontrollable urge to do so.
This eliminates conflict between your personal
passionate activity and other important activities in
your life. Immerse yourself in your favoured activity
whenever you get the chance to do so. Fully focused
on what you are doing, you can flow. When you have
to spend time doing other necessary tasks, you can
adapt and give them proper attention without feeling
resentful. So harmonious passion, rather than
obsessive passion, is conducive to ikigai.

SEEK OUT THE RIGHT PEOPLE

Sometimes you need to look beyond your inner circle to connect with others who share your particular passion. Take the example of the globally renowned chef Jason Atherton. His journey to the top of his profession included a literal climb to seek experience at the legendary Michelin three-star elBulli restaurant, in Spain. After sleeping on a beach because he didn't have enough money for a hotel, he borrowed a bicycle to cycle through the mountains to get there. He arrived exhausted and drenched in sweat, but impressed with his efforts, the elBulli management gave him a job. Since then Atherton has headed up multiple Michelin-star restaurants around the world himself.

OBJECTS OF VALUE

Finding meaning in the every day can extend to objects. Consider the classic American sitcom *Frasier*. The series begins with ex-cop Martin Crane, retired after being shot in the hip, moving in to the plush Seattle apartment of his highly cultured, psychiatrist son Frasier. To Frasier's horror, Martin brings with him a ragged armchair, held together by duct tape, which he plonks down in the centre of the tastefully furnished living room.

Frasier cannot fathom why anyone would keep this monstrosity. It is only in a later episode, when workmen carelessly throw the chair away, that Martin explains why he loves it. It was where he watched Neil Armstrong take the first step on the Moon and the US hockey team

beat the Russians in the 1980 Olympics, he tells Frasier. It was where he was sitting the night Frasier called to tell him he was going to be a grandfather. And, even more poignantly, his beloved late wife (and Frasier's mother) used to wake him up with a kiss when he'd fallen asleep in the chair. 'You know, I still fall asleep in it', he says. 'And every once in a while, when I wake up, I still expect your mother to be there, ready to lead me off to bed. . .' Frasier finally appreciates that the chair, which is duly retrieved from the garbage, has great value and meaning.

So ikigai may be about living in the present, but that doesn't mean you lose your memory. Objects that remind you of meaningful moments in your life, of who and what you have loved, and continue to love, give context to your current endeavours.

When to let go

Following your ikigai requires passion and persistence, but if a passion becomes an unhealthy obsession there could be dire consequences. Whereas harmonious passion is flexible and allows space for self-development in other activities, obsessive passion is rigid and can smother the rest of your life. When you are seeking excellence in a certain area, it is easy for your passion to slip into obsession, so be wary. If an activity that once brought you joy is now consistently causing upset to you and others, it's time to pull back and rebalance your priorities. It might even be time to let go and enjoy searching for a new passion.

FAMILIAL LOVE

In 1969, Japanese actor, radio and TV personality, and author, Musei Tokugawa, was interviewed by *Kosei* magazine. By then, 74 years old and in failing health, Tokugawa spoke warmly of his two grandchildren, aged four and three. 'I will never live long enough to have these children take care of me,' he said. 'My loving and looking after them are entirely a one-way activity. Probably I'll soon have to leave this world . . . And when the time comes to say goodbye forever, I'll be brimming with the happiness they gave me.' Yet, his interactions with his grandchildren really weren't a 'one-way activity'. In return for Tokugawa's love and care, they gave him the most valuable gift: a life worth living until his final breath.

4

WHAT THE WORLD NEEDS

Our actions cause ripples that spread and touch other people and affect the environment, so seek personal fulfilment in harmony with the wider world.

FREEDOM WITH RESPONSIBILITY

In Japanese culture, respect for other people and the natural world is an important aspect of ikigai. After all, if everyone focused purely on fulfilling their own desires, some fundamental needs of society and the environment would likely be neglected. Equally, it is understood that a strong society and sustainable environment creates a firmer foundation for individuals to explore deeply personal ambitions. The trick is to find time for activities that both inspire you and contribute to the greater good, whether that is in nature and wildlife conservation or charitable work for needy people.

❝ It is through our participation with others, sharing experiences with them or acting together with them for a common purpose that we obtain our highest sense of value of experience. ❞

———

Hadley Cantril, psychology professor,
Princeton University, 1950

Half a dozen ways to care

Pursuing your personal ikigai at times when your overriding priority is the welfare of others can be very challenging. A 2002 study by Noriko Yamamoto-Mitani and Margaret Wallhagen asked how Japanese caregivers to elderly parents with dementia tried to do so in the most testing of circumstances. Those who adapted easily to the caring role, or strongly believed in the value of what they were doing, reported that ikigai was not at the forefront of their minds. 'Because I devote myself to accomplish everything, I lose myself in them,' said Mayu, 56, 'I have not time for pondering about such things as ikigai.' Ironically, Mayu was describing the flow state – subconsciously she has ikigai.

For others though, the pressures of caregiving led them consciously to attempt to maintain or restore ikigai in six main ways. First, many caregivers cited family harmony and health – for instance, the satisfaction of seeing their children grow up – as a driving force for them to cope with the difficulties of care-giving. Ikigai was also maintained by balancing multiple different roles successfully. For Naoko, 42, making time to continue her English classes motivated her to fulfil her responsibilities as a caregiver. A third way was finding substitute activities for those given up due to the demands of care. Rie, 58, spent spare time while with her elderly parent making clothes.

'I cannot dress up and go out now, but I can let my daughter have some nice clothes,' she said.

'That is one ikigai.'

The fourth strategy was described by the researchers as 'intentional perceptual modification', where people accepted they had no choice but to be a carer in the circumstances, and almost forced themselves to believe that life was okay. 'I have to believe that taking care of my mother is my ikigai, otherwise I feel empty,' said Emi, 51. Ikigai was also maintained in philosophy and religious belief. Reiko, 57, a Christian who put a successful career on hold to care for her mother, rationalised the situation, saying: 'I don't think it really matters to a person whether one can or cannot do something.' When caregiving was so demanding as to leave no time for anything else, the sixth strategy involved maintaining ikigai by daydreaming of future freedom from responsibility and this helped offer more love and care in the here and now.

BEACON
OF LIGHT

In the 1931 novel *Night Flight* by Antoine de Saint-Exupéry, the glow from an oil lamp in the window of a lone house up in the mountains helps an aeroplane pilot to avoid crashing. In the days before the invention of radar, the occupier of this remote dwelling unwittingly saved the pilot's life. Japanese writer Tsuyako Miyake saw this story as analogous to how little things that we think we are doing just for ourselves may be vital to a total stranger. 'We are all doing something for countless strangers and countless strangers are doing something for us,' she commented in 1969. 'I try to keep this in mind always.' Imagine, then, the impact you can make when you actively seek to serve others in ways aligned to your personal ikigai. Let your light shine.

Ask for help

Just as you may nourish a profound personal sense of
fulfilment through helping others, be aware that other
people can derive similar benefits from assisting you.
So do not be afraid to ask those with greater knowledge
in a certain area for guidance. You may learn valuable
lessons. Equally, by taking an interest in their personal
experiences, you may enhance their feelings that
those experiences are valuable and consolidate
their own sense of purpose in life.

Spread the love

In March 2011, a massive earthquake occurred in
eastern Japan triggering a tsunami and devastating
cities across a huge area. Ikigai was shown to help people
to deal with physical and psychological trauma in the
aftermath. A restaurateur whose businesses were
destroyed in the tsunami, opened a tiny ramen shop
with the simple goal to make people eat, drink and
smile again. Another survivor kept a diary in the firm
belief that describing the events relating to the
earthquake would help people in future. Such people
giving back in different ways inspired others to give
of themselves. Thus a sense of purpose was re-
established both for individuals and communities
as a whole. Love spreads, and so does ikigai.

Express your
appreciation

———

When you are following your ikigai, the need
for validation and recognition from other people
diminishes in importance. However, it remains true that
all humans are emotional creatures and our behaviour,
attitude and general outlook on life are affected to a
greater or lesser extent by how people treat us. So be
considerate in your interactions with others. Be generous
in expressing your gratitude for their efforts. In doing so,
you may help them discover their ikigai; something they
can offer that the world needs, a quality they possess
that perhaps they hadn't previously realised because
it had never been acknowledged before.

VIRTUAL
CONNECTION

The confluence of what the world needs and what you love speaks to your mission. But if the structure and prevailing values of the society in which you live do not coincide with your own, you may find it difficult to follow your ikigai. This is where the virtual world, rather than being a distraction from your search for meaning in the real world, can assist you. Via the internet, information on almost any subject is readily available for you to explore and it is easier than ever to connect with like-minded people who you can assist and who can help you. Technology is shrinking the world, so use it with intent to find your mission.

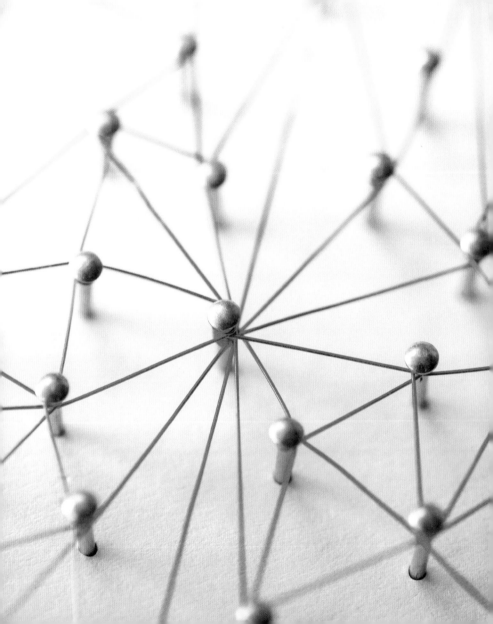

> **'Even small acts
> of compassion bring
> meaning and purpose
> to our lives.'**

———

Oscar Wilde, poet and playwright

The importance of listening

How will you understand what the world needs if you don't listen? It is easy to lock yourself in an echo chamber, interacting only with those who share, and thus reinforce, your opinions. This can lead to conflicts that defy all reason. Reach out to those who your actions affect. Listen to their concerns. Maybe you can adapt and still maintain your purpose while building more harmonious relationships. Their feedback may even open up hitherto unimagined opportunities for mutual benefit.

5

WHAT YOU CAN BE PAID FOR

The personal value to you of a job or career
cannot be measured purely in money earned,
so aim for work that enriches your life.

THE SECRET?

It seems that a career built on the principles of ikigai can be the secret to a happy working life. A typical Japanese worker is said to be highly motivated and quick to take action, is driven by teamwork rather than self-interest, and thrives on being thanked for their hard work. The conclusion: if you feel your work makes a positive difference, you've probably found your ikigai.

‘ If you are working on something exciting that you really care about, you don't have to be pushed. The vision pulls you. ’

———

Steve Jobs, entrepreneur

Work isn't everything

Your job should allow you to maintain other ikigai
outside of work. In Japan, there is a long-held corporate
culture of expecting employees to work extremely long
hours. So, while the Japanese may have found the secret
to a happy working life in the ikigai philosophy, some
companies' exploitation of workers makes it impossible to
realise. The key is for your work to represent just one
among several ikigai in a rich tapestry that gives
meaning to your life. If you find your work is
suffocating all your other interests,
it is time to make a change.

THE REWARD GAP

———

Pursuing a new career path does not necessarily yield immediate financial rewards and this can cause people to give up prematurely. Finding ikigai in the daily process of doing can help to sustain you on the journey. So long as you love what you do, and can find some means to continue, the daily experience may enrich your life beyond any monetary considerations. Just because your work isn't highly valued in the marketplace doesn't mean that it isn't valuable to you.

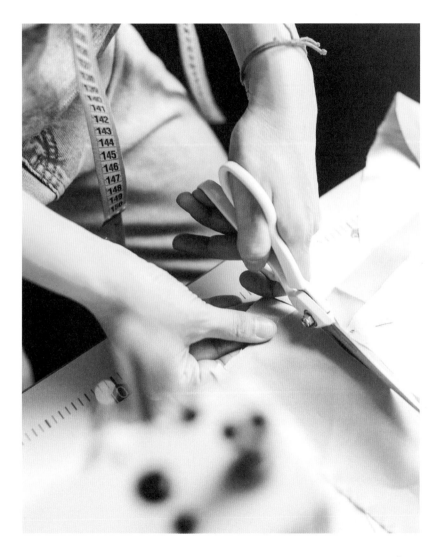

" An ikigai, in some ways, is like a compass ... As your career evolves and you're presented with more opportunities, you can rely on your ikigai to steer you in the right direction. "

Melody Wilding, high-performance coach

Build your *moai*

———

Embarking on a new career path can be very daunting, so it is important to have a support network as you follow your ikigai. Borrow from the people of Okinawa, who have a *moai* system whereby everyone is assigned a little 'club' of friends from birth who stay with them throughout their lives. The support of their *moai* is regarded as a key factor in the long and happy lives enjoyed by Okinawans. To guide you in your nascent career, look to build your own little *moai*, including expert mentors in your new field, people you meet who are taking a similar path and you find a personal connection with and valued friends, all of whom support your exploits in their own ways.

RELAX

———

After some consideration, you may conclude that while your job is not your ikigai, there are compelling reasons to continue nonetheless. Perhaps it helps you to maintain other ikigai, for example by financing hobbies, supporting your children in their passions or allowing you to contribute to causes close to your heart. Or maybe you just don't feel strong enough to make a change at this time. Relax – there is nothing wrong with appreciating what you've got. Simply remain mindful of the possibilities.

Making the best
of what you've got

If changing career direction is not an option, think
carefully about how your working life is now. Consider
all the elements, for example: the journey to and from
work; your working environment; the colleagues, clients
and customers you interact with; the daily routines; the
challenges you face; how you spend your break times;
whether you need a new briefcase; any social activities
related to work, and so on. Which parts make you feel
good? What could you do better? Do any activities
engage you sufficiently to get you into the flow state
where you lose track of time? Can you affect change
where you do more of the things you enjoy?

' Every job is good if you
do your best and work hard.
A man who works hard stinks
only to the ones that have
nothing to do but smell. '

———

Laura Ingalls Wilder, author
of *Little House on the Prairie*

WHITHER RETIREMENT?

In many countries, retirement is a rite of passage. Suddenly, you become an 'unproductive' member of society and if work was your ikigai, your main reason for getting up in the morning, this adjustment can be particularly difficult. The local dialect in Okinawa doesn't have a word for retirement. There, you find people like the hundred-year-old fisherman who still catches fish for his family three times per week. A statutory retirement age may prevent you continuing in your own job, but doing some form of work can help you to sustain your ikigai in later life.

6

WHAT
YOU ARE
GOOD AT

Give full expression to your skills, uncover
previously hidden talents and seek mastery
in everything you apply yourself to.

ATTENTION
TO DETAIL

———

A natural aptitude for a particular activity will take you so far, but to fulfil your potential requires extra commitment. Once you reach a high level of competence, it is harder to make improvements and any advances are less marked. The Japanese concept of *kodawari* can help in this respect. *Kodawari* describes a very personal attitude of taking great pride in everything you do and paying attention to the smallest details. Slight adjustments you make may or may not be noticed by others – but your efforts are never wasted. Being endlessly inquisitive and insistent on the highest standards will expedite your search for ikigai.

    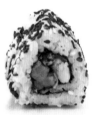

> **'** If you are going to achieve excellence in big things, you develop the habit in little matters. Excellence is not an exception, it is a prevailing attitude. **'**

Colin Powell, American statesman

Win when you are losing

We live in a competitive world in which a sharp line is often drawn between winners and losers. The beauty of ikigai is that 'winning' is something everybody can achieve. It is within your scope to find a niche that offers you an inner sense of satisfaction, regardless of structural measures of success or failure.

Is a sportsperson who attains the high level of proficiency required to become a professional player, loves what they do and continues to improve through their career, but never manages to win a tournament 'a loser'? Pay attention to your inner voice and define success on your own terms. None of us are winners or losers; we are all just human.

OTHER VOICES

Although locating your ikigai is ultimately your own very personal business, seeking the opinions of those who know you well may expedite your journey. Sometimes the things that are most familiar to us we take for granted, even our own abilities. Ask trusted friends, family members or work colleagues what they think are your best qualities. What they say might simply reinforce your own instinct and give you more confidence to follow it. But perhaps their comments will surprise you by highlighting an attribute you had underplayed and it will open your mind to new possibilities.

Failure is the
best way to learn

———

Just because you are good at something doesn't mean
you won't fail. In fact, if you challenge your ability,
failure is inevitable. The legendary inventor Thomas
Edison once said: 'I have not failed. I have found 10,000
ways that won't work.' Michael Jordan, one of the
greatest basketball players of all time admitted,
'I've failed over and over and over again in my life.
And that is why I succeed.' The Japanese have a saying:
Shippai wa seikou no moto, meaning 'failure is the
foundation of success.' So long as you learn from it,
failure can be your friend on your ikigai journey.

MASTERY

———

Ikigai is linked to a sense of mastery. By choosing options
that deeply motivate you, you will be imbued with the
energy and discipline required to make the most of your
ability. Whatever the task you set yourself, consistent,
concentrated application to every step of the process
will give you the greatest chance of excelling. Once
you have experienced the satisfaction that comes from
chanto suru – doing things properly – carry the same
rigour into all aspects of your life.

6 We do not act
rightly because we have
virtue or excellence, but
we rather have those because
we have acted rightly. We
are what we repeatedly do.
Excellence, then, is not
an act but a habit. 9

———

Aristotle, ancient Greek philosopher

Nothing is too simple

———

Remember that your ikigai does not have to be something ostentatious. It may be that your talents lie in performing more humble, everyday tasks that might not inspire awe in others, but are still valuable. Perhaps you are a good organiser of people, which allows them to make the most of their time. Or you are an empathetic listener who is always available to lend a friendly ear. You might not be a leader by nature, but still be an able member of the supporting cast. Doing ostensibly simple things well can be fulfilling.

7

FINDING YOUR IKIGAI

Discover the practical ways in which you can balance passion, mission, vocation and profession in order to foster and maintain ikigai in your life.

Get the balance right

If you focus only on your true passion, but cannot make enough money to survive doing that activity, it will be unsustainable. Similarly, concentrating on what you can be paid well for may bring you material wealth, but leave you feeling spiritually bereft. And if doing what you are good at doesn't seem to fit in with what your community and the wider world needs, that can also lead to a sense of isolation and lack of self-esteem. The ongoing challenge is to find and maintain a personally satisfying balance between your passion, mission, vocation and profession.

SOULSTORMING

———

A good starting point on your ikigai journey is to pick a
favorite notebook to use for soulstorming sessions.
Compile lists under four headings: What do you love?
What does the world need? What can you be paid for?
What are you good at? Scribble down any and all ideas
– there are no wrong answers. This is more than a
brainstorming; it requires you to access your deepest
desires in your heart and soul, which the strictures of life
may have suppressed. So allow yourself time. Tweak and
add to your lists over a period of days or weeks.

The Saturday morning test

Another way to tease out your ikigai is a simple test
advocated by author Neil Pasricha: what do you do
on Saturday morning if you have nothing to do?
Think for a minute then say your answer out loud.
Then brainstorm a list of ways you could pursue
other opportunities connected to this passion.
For example, you make beautiful cupcakes?
Share ideas with fellow bakers via social media;
teach at a local community centre; establish a product
range; offer your creations to local party planners.
'Your authentic self will be drawn to
these ideas,' says Pasricha.

CROSS-POLLINATION

In making four lists of your loves, skills, what you could earn money for and what world needs, you will see that some of your ideas might fit into two or more categories. This is the kind of cross-pollination you are looking for. To visualise this better, it is helpful to make your own ikigai Venn diagram (see page 25) and drop in each entry from your lists. Which things fall at the intersections between categories? Does anything satisfy all criteria? Most likely there will be unknowns – for instance, you might love something and have shown some aptitude for it, but whether you could earn money from it needs more investigation.

SUPPORTIVE IKIGAI

On your lists there are bound to be outliers that fit into just one of the four segments of the ikigai Venn diagram. Say you love sitting in the park watching the world go by, but can't make a case that it is something the world needs, involves any particular skill or you could be paid for. However, relaxing in the park regularly may give you time to reflect, think creatively and reinvigorate you. The importance of what could be described as 'supportive ikigai' should not be dismissed.

Take action

Let your ideas for new ventures marinate for a while. See which ones remain in your mind and heart as things you think and feel will be fulfilling. Then it is time to take action and find out if these truly are your ikigai. Intent is nothing without action. Those of you with few existing commitments or ties will find it easier to make a handbrake turn in your lives and test out more radical plans. For others it will necessarily be a more gradual process, but needn't be any less purposeful.

Make time

Early in your ikigai quest, strip out the dead wood. Stop doing the things that clearly don't fit into your new vision for your life, to free up as much time as possible to devote to the main priorities you have identified. Ring-fence time in your schedule so that you can really focus on your chosen activities. Only by creating that space to immerse yourself in new pursuits, will you be able to test properly that your initial instincts were correct.

BE BOLD

———

By shifting your priorities and opening yourself up to novel experiences, your ikigai will reveal itself to you. This may happen quickly, but it could take many months or years of trial and error. Be patient and enjoy the odyssey. Just engaging more fully with your inner self – and connecting with different people who share the same values – will enrich your daily life and strengthen your resolve. Then when a big decision has to be made, you can act boldly, safe in the knowledge that you are being completely true to yourself.

Revisit, refresh and revise

None of your ikigai are set in stone. Every now and again, revisit the notepad where you first wrote down your ideas and/or your personal ikigai Venn diagram. Have you faithfully followed the path you mapped out? Which items are more or less relevant? What is making you happiest and what is detrimental to your inner sense of well-being at the moment? Do you need to make minor adjustments or begin a more fundamental overhaul? Are you feeling fulfilled in your daily life? Refresh and revise accordingly.

" The truth is nobody
knows what they want
to do with their entire life.
Nobody ... Having one giant
purpose you strive toward
forever isn't the goal. "

———

Neil Pasricha, author

BANK OF IKIGAI

During our lives we are bound to experience traumas
that derail us – the break-up of a long-term relationship,
a bereavement, redundancy, a serious injury that
prevents you pursuing a favourite activity, and so on.
Suddenly, a central ikigai object is lost. When such
misfortune befalls you, it helps if you have built up a
bank of ikigai to draw upon; a treasure chest of small
things that have added useful purpose to your daily life
over previous years. These will not immediately fill the
void, or ever replace what you had, but together they may
help you get back on track. And, given time, one of these
may even come to the fore in your new reality.

Accept who you are

The ikigai philosophy is not about a one-size-fits-all solution. There is no list of commandments or rules to adhere to, no one prescribed route. Your ikigai is for you to discover within yourself as your life unfolds. By being open to trying new things, and by being more aware of how every experience makes you feel – and impacts upon others – you will gradually gain a better understanding of yourself and your place in the world.

EPILOGUE

You have learned that, with ikigai to guide you, every day becomes more meaningful, active and fulfilling. To recap on the eminent psychiatrist Mieko Kamiya's observation, finding value in life depends less on whether every ambition is realised than whether you purposefully take the direction that reflects your true nature.

There will likely be many things that you love, are good at, can be paid for and do to the benefit of the wider world. Not all that you do will meet all four criteria, but will contribute to your sense of value in life, nevertheless. If you are alive to the possibilities in each moment, you will discover multiple ikigai. Some will require more of your time and emotional energy, some will be frivolous, but each will add to your deep sense of purpose and joy in being.

It is heading in the direction that calls you and appreciating each step of the journey that is important; that is what will get you jumping out of bed each morning. So change your way of thinking. Be mindful of small things – things that perhaps you previously attached no significance to – and take pride in doing things properly.

Remember: whatever has happened before or may happen in the future, all that we have is now. There is a Japanese phrase *ichigo ichie* ('one time, one encounter'), which has its origins in the Japanese tea ceremony. It reminds those present that the ceremony they are having now will never be repeated. Even if the same group of people meets again in the same place on a different day, there will be many differences, so they must treasure this encounter as if it is their last and take pleasure in every detail.

This attitude underpins the ikigai philosophy and can help you live each day to the fullest. When you use all your senses, even daily routines that you previously found monotonous can come alive with meaning.

Life is happening now. Don't let it pass you by.

Recommended Reading

Books

Antonovsky, Aaron, *Health, Stress and Coping*, (Jossey-Bass Publishers, 1979)

Antonovsky, Aaron, *Unravelling the Mystery of Health: How People Manage Stress and Stay Well*, (Jossey-Bass Publishers, 1987)

Cantril, Hadley, *The 'Why' of Man's Experience*, (The Macmillan Company, 1950)

Csikszentmihaly, Mikhaly, *Finding Flow: The Psychology of Engagement With Everyday Life*

Csikszentmihaly, Mikhaly, *Flow: The Psychology of Happiness*

Delorie, Oliver Luke, *Wabi Sabi: Finding Beauty in Imperfection*, (Quarto Publishing, 2018)

García, Hector and Francesc Miralles, *Ikigai: The Japanese Secret to a Long and Happy Life*, (Penguin Books, 2017)

Maslow, Abraham H., *The Farther Reaches of Human Nature*, (The Viking Press, 1971)

Mathews, Gordon, and Carolina Izquierdo, Ed., *Pursuits of happiness: well-being in anthropological perspective* (Berghahn, 2009) – chapter by Gordon Mathews: 'Finding and keeping a purpose in life: well-being and Ikigai in Japan and elsewhere'

Mogi, Ken, *The Little Book of Ikigai: The Secret Japanese Way to Live a Happy and Long Life*, (Quercus, 2017)

Niwano, Nikkyō, *The Meaningful Life*, (First published 1969 in Japanese under the title *Ningen no Ikigai*, translated by Richard L. Gage, Kosei Publishing Co, Tokyo, First English Edition, 1982)

Ware, Bronnie, *The Top Five Regrets of the Dying*, (Hay House, 2011)

Journal articles

Demura, S, H. Kobayashi and T.Kitabayashi, "QOL Models Constructed for the Community-dwelling Elderly with Ikigai (purpose in life) as a Composition Factor, and the Effect of Habitual Exercise," (*Journal of Physiological Anthropology and Applied Human Science, Vol. 24, No. 5, 2005, Japan Society of Physiological Anthropology*)

Iida, K. and Y. Oguma, "Relationships Between Flow Experience, IKIGAI, and Sense of Coherence in Tai Chi Practitioners," (*Holistic Nursing Practice*, Vol. 27. No. 5, 2013)

Mathews, Gordon, "Ikigai: Contemporary Japanese Conceptions of What Makes Life Worth Living," (Abstracts of the Annual

Meeting of the Association for Asian Studies, Los Angeles, CA, 1993)

Mathews, Gordon, "The Pursuit of a Life Worth Living in Japan and the United States," (*Ethnology*, Vol. 35, No. 1, Winter 1996)

Mitani, Noriko and Wallhagen, Margaret I., "Pursuit of Psychological Well-Being (Ikigai) and the Evolution of Self-Understanding in the Context of Caregiving in Japan," (*Culture, Medicine and Psychiatry*, Vol. 26; No.4 ; 2002)

Mori, Ken et al., "Sense of life worth living (ikigai) and incident functional disability in elderly Japanese: The Tsurugaya Project," (*Journal of Psychosomatic Research* 95, February 2017)

Nakanishi, Noriyuki, '"Ikigai" in Older Japanese People,' (Age and Ageing, 28: 323-324, 1999)

Tanno, K. et al., 'Associations of ikigai as a positive psychological factor with all-cause mortality and cause-specific mortality among middle-aged and elderly Japanese people: Findings from the Japan Collaborative Cohort Study,' (*Journal of Psychosomatic Research*, Vol. 67, No. 1, 2009)

Vallerand, Robert J., "On the Psychology of Passion: In Search of What Makes People's Lives Most Worth Living," (*Canadian Psychology*, Vol. 49, No. 1, 2008)

Online articles

Buettner, Dan, *How to Live to be 100*, (ted.com/ talks, January 2010)

Carlyle, Rachel, *Move over Scandi! We want to Live the Ikigai Life Now*, (thetimes.co.uk, August 12, 2017)

Gander, Kashmira, *Is Ikigai the New Hygge? The Japanese Concept of Finding Purpose in our Lives*, (independent.co.uk, September 19, 2017)

Kavedžija, Iza, *The Japanese Concept of Ikigai: Why Purpose Might be a Better Goal Than Happiness*, (theconversation.com, December 2017)

Joshi, Kohei, *A Beautiful World Through Five Traditional Japanese Concepts*, (theodysseyonline.com, November 30, 2015)

Mitsuhashi, Yukari, Ikigai: *A Japanese Concept to Improve Work and Life*, (bbc.com, August 2, 2017)

Oliver, Laura, *Is this Japanese concept the secret to a long, happy, meaningful life?*, (weforum.org, August 9, 2017)

Oliver, Laura, *The Japanese Concept of Ikigai Could be the Secret to a Long, Meaningful Life*, (uk.businessinsider.com, September 16, 2017)

Ough, Tom, *Finding your Ikigai: the Japanese Secret to Health and Happiness*, (telegraph. co.uk, July 16, 2017)

Pasricha, Neil, *Find your Passion by Taking this Test*, (thestar.com, 10 January 10, 2017)

Ramalho, Marina, *Four Japanese Concept to Apply to Your Life in 2017*, (joyofless.ca, December 17, 2016)

Wilding, Melody, *The Japanese Concept 'Ikigai' is a Formula for Happiness and Meaning*, (betterhumans.coach.me, November 30, 2017)

Winn, Marc, *What is your Ikigai?*, (theviewinside.me, May 14, 2014)